MW01257119

BECOMING

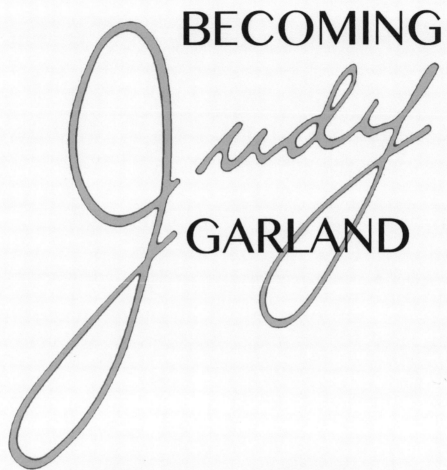

Judy

GARLAND

Randy L. Schmidt

TRIBAL CLEF BOOKS

To the students of
Dorothy P. Adkins Elementary
Lantana, Texas

"We are the music makers
and we are the dreamers of dreams"

Tribal Clef Books, Denton, Texas
© 2017 Randy L. Schmidt All rights reserved.
ISBN: 978-0-9995888-0-2 (Hardcover)

JUDY GARLAND was
born Frances Ethel
Gumm on June 10,
1922, in Grand Rapids,
Minnesota.

The world fell in love
with her as "Dorothy"
in *The Wizard of Oz*,
the 1939 M-G-M
classic, one of the most
beloved films of all time. She went on to become one of
the greatest entertainers in show business history.
This is her story.

4

FRANK AND ETHEL GUMM were vaudeville entertainers. They trouped from town to city with fellow actors, comedians, dancers, magicians, and singers. The couple eventually made their home and started a family in Grand Rapids.

Mr. Gumm managed a local theater and his wife played piano during silent movies. Between films, daughters Mary Jane and Virginia danced and sang together as "The Gumm Sisters," a family vaudeville act.

IT WAS CHRISTMASTIME 1924 when two-year-old Frances, the youngest daughter, made her debut on the stage of her father's theater. She sang "Jingle Bells" and the crowd responded with a thunderous ovation.

Frances loved the sound of the applause and cheers so much that she wouldn't stop singing. Mr. Gumm finally had to carry her off the stage kicking and screaming!

8

THE REVIEWS WERE IN: Frances Gumm was a big hit! A local newspaper reported her singing was a "genuine surprise."

With the new nickname "Baby" Gumm, Frances joined the sister act. The trio performed at the theater, around town, and even at home for family and friends. They put on a show anytime and anyplace somebody sat still long enough to watch.

THE FAMILY'S TIME IN MINNESOTA was short-lived. When Frances was four, they sold their house and headed west for sunny Southern California.

The Gumm Sisters spent several months playing one-nighters in just about every major city along the way. The family finally settled in Antelope Valley, California, north of Los Angeles in the Mojave Desert.

12

MR. GUMM CONTINUED TO MANAGE movie theaters, while his wife earned a reputation as an aggressive stage mother. Mrs. Gumm detested the desert and soon moved the girls to Hollywood.

Mary Jane and Virginia lost interest in performing and wanted to quit. By then, "Baby" Frances was the star of the act anyway. She may have been small, but her voice certainly wasn't. People marveled at her power and called her the "little girl with the BIG voice."

THE GUMM SISTERS went on one final tour together in the summer of 1934. They all piled into the family car and headed east for the Chicago World's Fair.

A theater manager in the Windy City promised the girls would see their name up in electric lights.
But when they arrived, it wasn't "The Gumm Sisters" they saw blinking brightly overhead. Instead, it said, "THE GLUMM SISTERS."

THE EMCEE THAT NIGHT WAS GEORGE JESSEL, a popular comedian. He told Frances she was "as pretty as a garland of roses" and suggested the girls change their name to "The Garland Sisters."

Frances declared she wanted a new first name, too. So it was then and there, backstage at the Oriental Theatre in Chicago, the Gumm Sisters became the Garland Sisters. And Frances Gumm became Judy Garland.

A TALENT AGENT HEARD JUDY SING and offered to take her around Hollywood to audition for several movie studios.

She sang for Louis B. Mayer, the head of Metro-Goldwyn-Mayer, better known as M-G-M. He and the others liked Judy so much that they signed her to a movie contract in 1935. At first, the studio was not quite sure what to do with her. Judy was an "in-between." Too old to be a kid, but too young to be an adult.

JUDY REPORTED TO HER FIRST DAY OF WORK
at M-G-M and, much to her surprise, was sent
straight to school.

There were a half-dozen other child actors on the
studio lot. Like Judy, several of the others, including
Jackie Cooper and Mickey Rooney, got their start in
vaudeville and were also making the transition
into movies. They all attended daily classes together at
M-G-M's Little Red Schoolhouse, which was
curiously painted white.

WHEN JUDY'S FATHER SUDDENLY BECAME ILL
and was hospitalized, she was preparing to sing for a live radio show.

The family doctor called Judy just before the performance to say that Mr. Gumm would be listening from his hospital bed. She sang "Zing! Went the Strings of My Heart" especially for him that night, but by morning he was gone.

RETURNING TO WORK after the death of her father wasn't easy, but Judy remained busy at the studio. She was paired with Mickey Rooney in several films, but mostly entertained for parties and special events on the M-G-M lot.

For a birthday celebration honoring her favorite actor, Clark Gable, Judy sang "Dear Mr. Gable: You Made Me Love You." In return, he gave her a charm bracelet engraved: *To My Best Girl, Judy—from Clark Gable.*

WHEN JUDY WAS 15, M-G-M purchased the film rights to L. Frank Baum's book, *The Wonderful Wizard of Oz.*

It was always meant to be a showcase for Judy, but rumors surfaced that "America's Sweetheart" might get the part. Shirley Temple was the most popular child star of the late 1930s. But Judy's singing ability and unrivaled talent set her apart. She was the obvious and only choice for the role of "Dorothy."

SONGS FOR *THE WIZARD OF OZ* were all written with Judy in mind. Her heartfelt performance of "Over the Rainbow" helped the song win the Academy Award for "Best Original Song" in 1940.

After *Oz*, Judy was hailed as one of most famous movie stars in the world. "Over the Rainbow" became her signature tune and one of the most enduring songs of the 20th century. Both the movie and the song will forever be identified with Judy Garland.

JUDY GARLAND
(June 10, 1922 - June 22, 1969)

Throughout her career, Judy Garland was known as
"Miss Show Business." And it's no wonder! She made
32 feature films, hosted four network television specials,
taped a 26-episode series for CBS-TV, made countless
TV guest appearances, recorded nearly 100 singles and
more than a dozen studio albums, appeared on hundreds
of radio shows, and made upward of 1,500 live
concert appearances.

Despite achieving fame and bringing so much joy to
others, Judy's life was not always a happy one. She had a strained
relationship with her mother, who was often demanding and overbearing. But it was
the absence of her father that brought Judy the most agony during her teenage years.
The sudden death of Frank Gumm seemed to signal the end of Frances Gumm. "I don't
associate Frances Gumm with me," Judy said in 1951. "She's a girl I can read about the
way other people do. I, Judy Garland, was born when I was twelve years old."

As an adult, Judy was the devoted mother to three children: Liza Minnelli, Lorna Luft,
and Joe Luft. Unlucky in love, she married five times. Throughout much of her life,
Judy suffered from an addiction to prescription drugs, rooted in her early years in
Hollywood. While working for M-G-M, she became dependent upon various
medications to keep up with the studio's demands. On June 22, 1969, Judy Garland
died in London of an accidental overdose of sleeping pills. She was 47.

The Judy Garland Show, Carnegie Hall, *A Star is Born*, The Palace, The Palladium,
Easter Parade, Meet Me in St. Louis . . . These career highlights alone would qualify
an entertainer for legend status. But then there is *The Wizard of Oz*. The Library of
Congress says it's "the most watched film ever," and it was *Oz* that elevated Judy from
"legend" to the realm of immortality. When Judy as "Dorothy" opened the door to
that glorious land, donned a pair of magical ruby slippers, and skipped down the
Yellow Brick Road, she took with her generations of youngsters and the young at
heart who will always believe there's no place like home.

Recommended Listening:

"Zing! Went the Strings of My Heart"
"Dear Mr. Gable: You Made Me Love You"
"Over the Rainbow"
"The Boy Next Door"
"The Trolley Song"
"Have Yourself a Merry Little Christmas"
"A Couple of Swells"
"Get Happy"
"The Man That Got Away"
"Smile"

Recommended Reading:

The Wonderful Wizard of Oz by L. Frank Baum
The Wizard of Oz: The Official 75th Anniversary Companion
by Jay Scarfone and William Stillman
Judy Garland on Judy Garland: Interviews and Encounters by Randy L. Schmidt

About the Author:

RANDY L. SCHMIDT is a music educator and author of the critically-acclaimed *Little Girl Blue: The Life of Karen Carpenter*, a *New York Times* Editor's Choice and *Wall Street Journal* Best Seller. He also compiled and edited *Yesterday Once More: The Carpenters Reader*, *Judy Garland on Judy Garland: Interviews and Encounters*, and *Dolly on Dolly: Interviews and Encounters with Dolly Parton*. He resides in Denton, Texas.

Visit **randylschmidt.com** for more information.

NOTE: Special editions of this book may include an Audiobook CD with extras, including rare 1935 Decca test recordings. These are used by permission of JSP Records, John H. Haley, and Lawrence Schulman, and can also be found on *Best of Lost Tracks* (JSP Records, 2015).

CREDITS

Photos courtesy of:
Archive Photos,
Globe Photos,
International Judy Garland Club
(judygarlandclub.org),
Itasca County Historical Society
(itascahistorical.org),
and Photofest

Art direction & layout:
kennyholcombdesigns.com

CPSIA information can be obtained at www.ICGtesting.com
Printed in the USA
BVIW12n1217291117
501544BV00005B/70